DINOS VS MACHINES

Written by Eric Geron
Illustrated by Mat Edwards

Prepare for Battle!

TEAM DINOSAUR – ROSTER LINE-UP

Millions of years later the dinos are back and ready to make up for lost time!

VELOCIRAPTOR

SPINOSAURUS

ARGENTINOSAURUS

ICHTHYOSAUR

TRICERATOPS

ANKYLOSAURUS

STEGOSAURUS

EDMONTOSAURUS

QUETZALCOATLUS

T. REX

Witness the most sensational smackdowns in the history of time as the greatest beasts who ever roamed go face-to-face with the mightiest machines ever invented in unprecedented contests and clashes for the ages!

Maaaaaake some noise for your stone-cold competitors!

TEAM MACHINE – ROSTER LINE-UP

Machines were built to help—but now they're ready to destroy!

 MOTORCYCLE

 TANK

 GARBAGE TRUCK

 SUBMARINE

 BULLDOZER

 CRANE

 EXCAVATOR

 SNOWMOBILE

 HELICOPTER

 MONSTER TRUCK

VELOCIRAPTOR

BATTLE STATS

TIME PERIOD: Late Cretaceous

LOCATION: Mongolia and China

DIET: Amphibians, reptiles, insects, small dinosaurs

HEIGHT: Up to 3.5 ft (1 m)

WEIGHT: Up to 33 lbs (15 kg)

LENGTH: Up to 6 ft (1.8 m)

Velociraptor is a fast, powerful, and smart predator. It's hungry to race—and will spring ahead to rip its opponent to shreds!

MOTORCYCLE

BATTLE STATS

CREATED IN: 1885

FOUND ON: Roads and highways

USED FOR: Traveling and racing

HEIGHT: Up to 4 ft (1.2 m)

WEIGHT: Up to 700 lbs (318 kg)

LENGTH: Up to 6 feet (1.8 m)

You can hear a powerful growl coming at you from down the road—and before you know it, you're left in a cloud of dust. What could it be? The miiiiiiiighty Motorcycle!

VELOCIRAPTOR VS. MOTORCYCLE

Here come two fierce forces of velocity and vigor! Of swiftness and speed! A round of applause for Velociraptor and Motorcycle as they go head-to-head in an obstacle course! Who will be crowned the winner, and who will lose steam before the finish? Aaand they're off!

Velociraptor jumps over its first hurdle with ease. Talk about catching air!

Motorcycle ducks under the hurdle. Nice slide! And it takes the lead!

The balance beam is no match for Motorcycle. It pops a wheelie!

But Velociraptor's right behind it now, using its tail for support.

ARGENTINOSAURUS

BATTLE STATS

TIME PERIOD: Late Cretaceous

LOCATION: Argentina

DIET: Plants

HEIGHT: Up to 70 ft (21 m)

WEIGHT: Up to 110 US ton (100 metric ton)

LENGTH: Up to 120 ft (37 m)

Argentinosaurus may be the most colossal dino ever! At the whopping height of seventy feet, you definitely wouldn't want to accidentally get in the path of this gentle giant! One little misstep could mean the end.

GARBAGE TRUCK

BATTLE STATS

CREATED IN: 1937

FOUND ON: Streets of cities and towns

USED FOR: Transporting garbage to landfills

HEIGHT: Up to 14 ft (4.3 m)

WEIGHT: Up to 13.4 US tons (12 metric tons)

LENGTH: Up to 12 ft (3.7 m

You can smell Garbage Truck before you see it. This stinky, trash-filled truck putters around town, filled with all the waste imaginable. It wastes no time getting its fill!

ARGENTINOSAURUS VS. GARBAGE TRUCK

Give a hearty welcome to our hungry friends: Argentinosaurus and Garbage Truck! Which champion eater will get through this feast of leafy greens first? 3 . . . 2 . . . 1 . . . Eat!

Argentinosaurus is off to an excellent start, and munches at a steady pace.

But Garbage Truck's mechanical arms quickly snatch up bins and start loading up!

Gulp! Argentinosaurus stops for a water break.

Garbage Truck is in the splash zone, and stops to wipe down its windshield.

They're munching again, until . . . oh no! Garbage Truck spits out trash from its rear—right at Argentinosaurus. Watch out!

Argentinosaurus is starting to feel full. Uh oh! Garbage Truck wasn't the only one who needed to empty out. Let that digest!

Argentinosaurus is ready to finish off its greens when Garbage Truck pinches its snout. Ouch! Can either of them get free?

AND THE **WINNER** IS . . .

?

Make your choice, then turn to page 44 to find out what the experts think!

TRICERATOPS

BATTLE STATS

TIME PERIOD: Late Cretaceous

LOCATION: North America

DIET: Plants

HEIGHT: Up to 10 ft (3 m)

WEIGHT: Up to 26,000 lbs (12,000 kg)

LENGTH: Up to 30 ft (9 m)

When Triceratops isn't munching low-lying plants, it's charging at its enemies with its pointy horns! This dino doesn't eat meat, but if it has *beef* with another dinosaur, or if a hungry predator gets up in its face, it's game on!

BULLDOZER

BATTLE STATS

CREATED IN: 1923

FOUND IN: Construction sites

USED FOR: Pushing sand, soil, and objects

HEIGHT: Up to 9 ft (2.7 m)

WEIGHT: Up to 42,000 lbs (19,000 kg)

LENGTH: Up to 22 ft (6.7 m)

This large, powerful machine isn't your average country tractor. With its blade, Bulldozer is meant for pushing and cutting soil, sand, or other materials. That's right, folks—Bulldozer can literally *move earth*.

13

TRICERATOPS VS. BULLDOZER

Let's take this wrestling match from the 'tops! This contest is going to be a real bull-doozy!

Triceratops makes the first move in the ring. It comes out charging with its horns low and runs at Bulldozer.

But Bulldozer lifts its blade to block the horns. Great save!

What's this? Triceratops is trying to take a bite out of Bulldozer! I'm not sure that's a legal move!

Triceratops can chew through plants like scissors, but its bite is no match for Bulldozer's steel.

Bulldozer is getting mad! Up goes its ripper. It's going to attack! But wait! Triceratops barrels forward and charges once more!

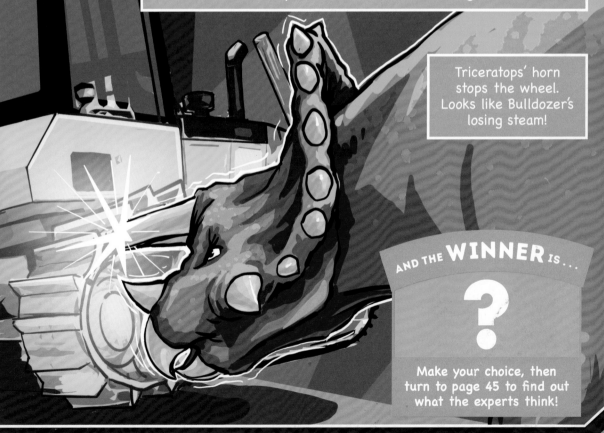

Triceratops' horn stops the wheel. Looks like Bulldozer's losing steam!

AND THE **WINNER** IS . . .

?

Make your choice, then turn to page 45 to find out what the experts think!

STEGOSAURUS

BATTLE STATS

TIME PERIOD: Late Jurassic

LOCATION: America, Madagascar, and Portugal

DIET: Plants

HEIGHT: Up to 9 ft (2.7 m)

WEIGHT: Up to 16,000 lbs (7,250 kg)

LENGTH: Up to 30 ft (9 m)

Recognized by the plates running down its back, Stegosaurus chomps vegetation and keeps to itself. When predators are hot on its trail, it swings its spiked tail to get them to back off.

EXCAVATOR

BATTLE STATS

CREATED IN: 1882

FOUND IN: Construction sites

USED FOR: Digging and hauling

HEIGHT: Up to 11 ft (3.5 m)

WEIGHT: Up to 80,000 lbs (36,000 kg)

LENGTH: Up to 11 ft (3.5 m)

Excavator boldly digs like no machine has before. It isn't afraid to bury its competition!

STEGOSAURUS VS. EXCAVATOR

It's time to see whether Stegosaurus or Excavator will dig to the bottom. Will Excavator step up to the plates? Will Stegosaurus eat dirt? Prepare to dig in!

Stegosaurus paws at its dirt pile, while Excavator's bucket chows down in one fell scoop!

Ha! Stegosaurus soils Excavator's plans when it swings its tail at it. That's playing dirty!

Stegosaurus stomps on top of Excavator's boom, which shakes under the strain of its weight. Excavator starts to tip. Dig it!

But who dug deep enough?

When Stegosaurus goes back to digging, it falls into the trench dug by Excavator!

AND THE **WINNER** IS . . .

?

Make your choice, then turn to page 45 to find out what the experts think!

QUETZALCOATLUS

BATTLE STATS

TIME PERIOD: Late Cretaceous

LOCATION: North America

DIET: Fish and dinosaurs

WINGSPAN: Up to 16.5 ft (5 m)

WEIGHT: Up to 550 lbs (250 kg)

LENGTH: Up to 33 ft (10 m)

If the giant shadow of the Quetzalcoatlus falls across your path—RUN! This flying reptile plunges from the skies with incredible speed to pluck up its victims in its enormous beak.

HELICOPTER

BATTLE STATS

CREATED IN: 1939

FOUND IN: Sky

USED FOR: Transportation and firefighting

HEIGHT: Up to 11 ft (3 m)

WEIGHT: Up to 16,000 lbs (7,250 kg)

LENGTH: Up to 11 ft (9 m)

Helicopter whirls through the sky with amazing grace, its blades spinning in a flash! Is it heading to put out a raging forest fire? Or is it revving up for an epic race through the air?

QUETZALCOATLUS VS. HELICOPTER

It's time for our contestants to take to the skies! Let the aerial race begin in the ultimate battle of fight or flight! Who will land on the distant cliffs first? Ready the clock . . . GO!

Helicopter takes the lead by zipping past Quetzalcoatlus in a blur and whir of blades!

But Quetzalcoatlus won't be beat so easily. It flies circles around Helicopter. Literally! Then it pounces.

Uh oh! Helicopter is a second too slow. Quetzalcoatlus chomps down on the chopper—and pierces a hole right in its fuel tank! Things are really spiraling out of control now!

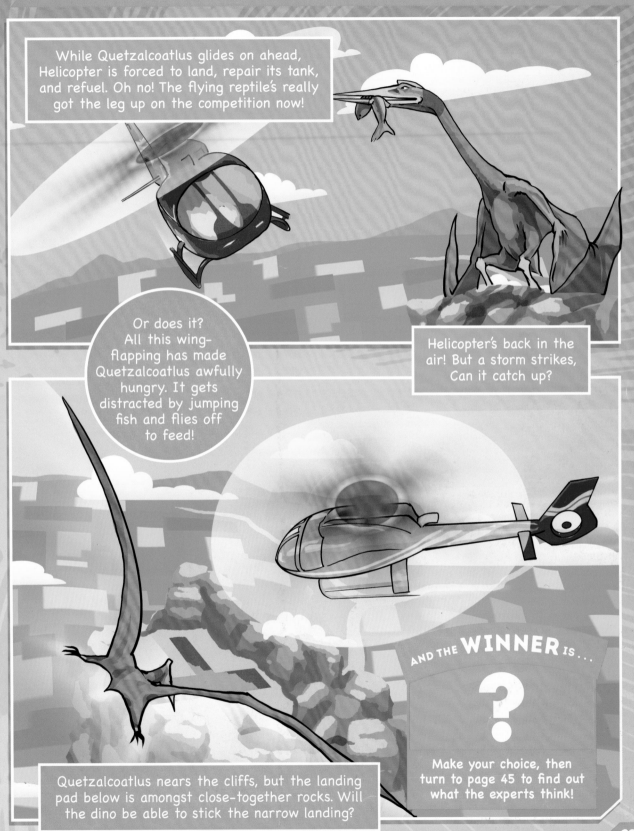

While Quetzalcoatlus glides on ahead, Helicopter is forced to land, repair its tank, and refuel. Oh no! The flying reptile's really got the leg up on the competition now!

Or does it? All this wing-flapping has made Quetzalcoatlus awfully hungry. It gets distracted by jumping fish and flies off to feed!

Helicopter's back in the air! But a storm strikes, Can it catch up?

Quetzalcoatlus nears the cliffs, but the landing pad below is amongst close-together rocks. Will the dino be able to stick the narrow landing?

AND THE **WINNER** IS . . .

?

Make your choice, then turn to page 45 to find out what the experts think!

SPINOSAURUS

BATTLE STATS

TIME PERIOD: Late Cretaceous

LOCATION: North Africa

DIET: Meat

HEIGHT: Up to 23 ft (7 m)

WEIGHT: Up to 46,000 lbs (21,000 kg)

LENGTH: Up to 50 ft (15 m)

When Spinosaurus isn't swimming the rivers to snag fish in its narrow mouth full of serrated teeth, it also walks on land—as the largest terrestrial carnivore to ever exist!

TANK

BATTLE STATS

CREATED IN: 1915

FOUND ON: Battlefields

USED FOR: Fighting

HEIGHT: Up to 8 ft (2.5 m)

WEIGHT: Up to 120,000 lbs (54,500 kg)

LENGTH: Up to 32 ft (9 m)

Tank rolls with speed to the front lines of battle, firing away with its forceful gun.

SPINOSAURUS VS. TANK

It's time! Introducing our mixed martial arts heavyweights! First to get knocked out wins! Will Spinosaurus tank its rival in the cage fight? On your claw marks . . . get set . . . go!

Spinosaurus squares up against Tank—and strikes.

Too bad Tank's armored side is impenetrable! Strike out!

Tank pivots its weapon to swing at Spinosaurus. Uh no!

Spinosaurus's tail thrashes it aside in time, saving its skin! Beast mode initiated!

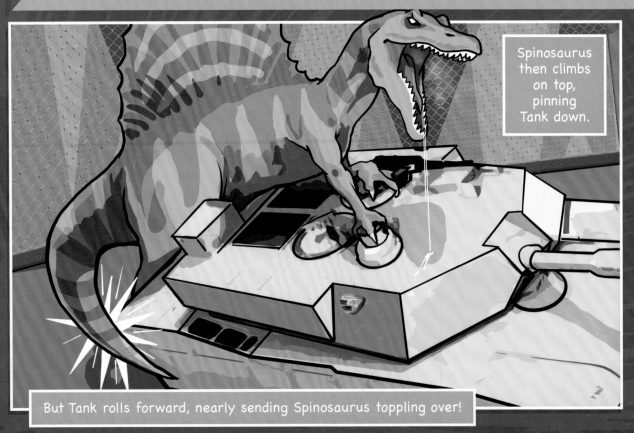

Spinosaurus then climbs on top, pinning Tank down.

But Tank rolls forward, nearly sending Spinosaurus toppling over!

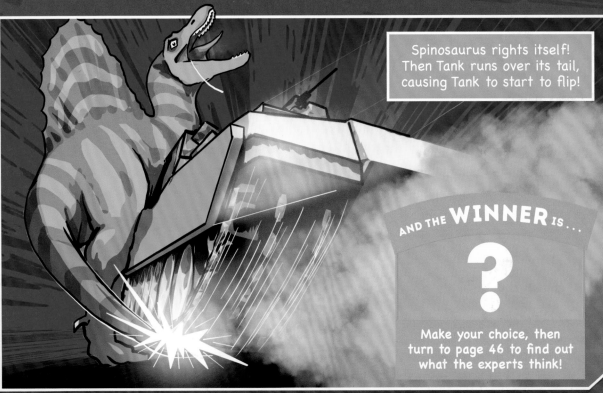

Spinosaurus rights itself! Then Tank runs over its tail, causing Tank to start to flip!

AND THE **WINNER** IS . . .

?

Make your choice, then turn to page 46 to find out what the experts think!

ICHTHYOSAUR

BATTLE STATS

TIME PERIOD: Early Triassic to Late Cretaceous

LOCATION: Ocean

DIET: Fish

HEIGHT: N/A

WEIGHT: Up to 2,000 lbs (900 kg)

LENGTH: Up to 82 ft (25 m)

This monster's sleek fin can be seen breaking through the surface of the sea. Its athletic flippers let it swim fast like a modern-day dolphin, and it can dive deep down to hunt fish.

SUBMARINE

BATTLE STATS

CREATED IN: 1620

FOUND IN: Ocean

USED FOR: Fighting, transportation, exploring

HEIGHT: Up to 40 ft (12 m)

WEIGHT: N/A

LENGTH: Up to 560 ft (170 m)

Submarine is a master of stealth! It dives far below the surface. When it's not exploring bodies of water sometimes too deep for divers, it may be cruising the depths . . . to destroy!

ICHTHYOSAUR VS. SUBMARINE

The ocean looks nice and clear today for our competitors to take a dive! In this deep battle, who will reach the ocean floor first? I've got a sinking feeling about this . . .

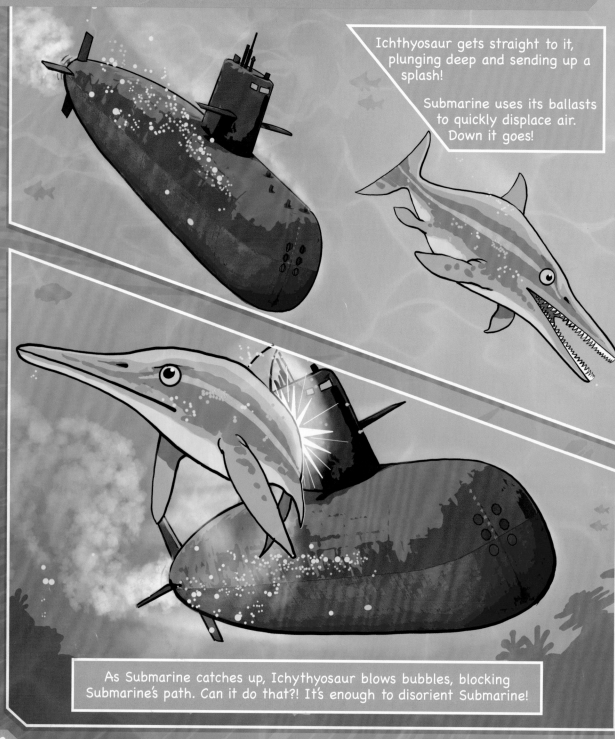

Ichthyosaur gets straight to it, plunging deep and sending up a splash!

Submarine uses its ballasts to quickly displace air. Down it goes!

As Submarine catches up, Ichythyosaur blows bubbles, blocking Submarine's path. Can it do that?! It's enough to disorient Submarine!

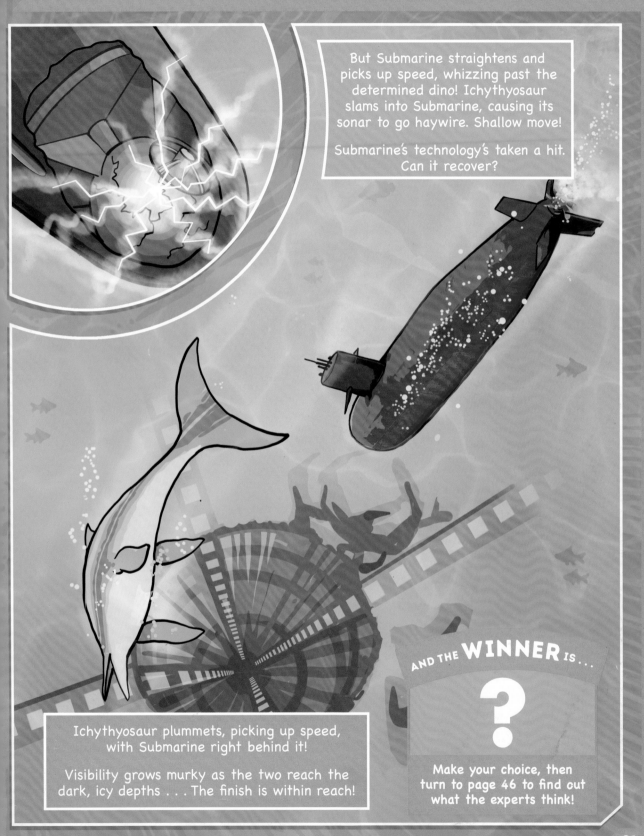

But Submarine straightens and picks up speed, whizzing past the determined dino! Ichythyosaur slams into Submarine, causing its sonar to go haywire. Shallow move!

Submarine's technology's taken a hit. Can it recover?

Ichythyosaur plummets, picking up speed, with Submarine right behind it!

Visibility grows murky as the two reach the dark, icy depths . . . The finish is within reach!

AND THE **WINNER** IS . . .

?

Make your choice, then turn to page 46 to find out what the experts think!

ANKYLOSAURUS

BATTLE STATS

TIME PERIOD: Late Cretaceous

LOCATION: North America

DIET: Plants

HEIGHT: Up to 4 ft (1.2 m)

WEIGHT: Up to 10,000 lbs (4,500 kg)

LENGTH: Up to 26 ft (8 m)

Ankylosaurus is a plant-eating dino who can fend for itself—in fact, it's equipped with horns, spikes, a tail club, and an armored body, making it a fierce contestant in any battle!

CRANE

BATTLE STATS

CREATED IN: 515 B.C.E.

FOUND IN: Construction sites

USED FOR: Lifting and moving objects

HEIGHT: Up to 265 ft (81 m)

WEIGHT: Up to 22,000 lbs (10,000 kg)

LENGTH: N/A

Crane lifts and moves objects to high, hard-to-reach places that require some muscle and precision. It also has a hook which can attach to a steel ball for maximum destruction.

ANKYLOSAURUS VS. CRANE

Let's give it up for Ankylosaurus and Crane! Who will be the first to annihilate their obstacles? Leeeet's get ready to crumble!

Crane takes a big swing with its wrecking ball at the brick. Whoa! Ankylosaurus whirls its clubbed tail and makes quick work of its wall!

Now they're onto cement. Crane wastes no time in demolishing it, but—oh no— Ankylosaurus is stuck!

It's time for the house! Crane has a lead, but here comes Ankylosaurus! The dino is using its arms and legs, too—is that cheating?

Crane is about to smash a car to pieces. This machine's got a lot of drive! But Ankylosaurus doesn't quit. It hurls itself at the car!

AND THE **WINNER** IS...

?

Make your choice, then turn to page 46 to find out what the experts think!

EDMONTOSAURUS

BATTLE STATS

TIME PERIOD: Late Cretaceous

LOCATION: North America

DIET: Plants

HEIGHT: Up to 10 ft (3 m)

WEIGHT: Up to 8,800 lbs (4,000 kg)

LENGTH: Up to 42 ft (13 m)

This duck-billed dino migrates in herds, grazing the ground for vegetation. It's not looking for any trouble. It may seem defenseless, but it'll put up a decent fight when it's do-or-die!

SNOWMOBILE

BATTLE STATS

CREATED IN: 1927

FOUND ON: Snow and ice

USED FOR: Racing and transportation

HEIGHT: Up to 4.5 ft (1.4 m)

WEIGHT: Up to 500 lbs (227 kg)

LENGTH: Up to 11 ft (3.3 m)

Snowmobile flies across snow and ice. It won't let a little cold weather get in its path!

EDMONTOSAURUS VS. SNOWMOBILE

It's real chilly weather here, everybody! Racers, warm up your engines! So now, which competitor will be the first to reach the finish line in a race of snow and ice? Let's find out!

Snowmobile rips through the snow in a blur! Uh oh! A blizzard's begun!

Edmontosaurus trots after it, using its keen sense of sight for visibility in the storm.

Snowmobile doesn't see a drop coming, and plunges down a slope!

It's stuck in a snow bank!

The dino finds itself on thin ice. It starts to crack. This can't be good! It'll need to take the long way around!

What's this? Snowmobile's back in the game and rumbles by. They've both made it across the frozen ice!

Snowmobile's almost to the finish when an avalanche dumps a pile of snow on its back! Edmontosaurus shakes free, but Snowmobile might be stuck!

AND THE **WINNER** IS . . .

?

Make your choice, then turn to page 47 to find out what the experts think!

T. REX

BATTLE STATS

TIME PERIOD: Late Cretaceous

LOCATION: North America

DIET: Meat

HEIGHT: Up to 20 ft (6 m)

WEIGHT: Up to 30,000 lbs (13,500 kg)

LENGTH: Up to 40 ft (12 m)

When T. rex isn't terrorizing the forests, it's terrorizing the swamps. Watch out for this fearsome meat-eater!

MONSTER TRUCK

BATTLE STATS

CREATED IN: 1979

FOUND IN: Stadiums and arenas

USED FOR: Racing and competing

HEIGHT: Up to 12 ft (3.6 m)

WEIGHT: Up to 12,000 lbs (5,500 kg)

LENGTH: Up to 17 ft (5.1 m)

This specialized truck races and competes in stadiums and arenas, soaring off ramps and dirt mounds, flipping deftly through the air, and popping wheelies with its oversized tires!

T. REX VS. MONSTER TRUCK

For a demolition derby like no other . . . here are . . . T. rex and Monster Truck! Time to feed their need to damage and destroy! Who'll wipe out their competition first? Let the derby bergin!

Monster Truck lets its engine roar and circles T. rex to try disorienting it!

But T. rex whips its sturdy tail, sending Monster Truck tumbling. This is pretty shattering to watch, folks!

Monster Truck doubles back around and flies off a dirt incline, aiming to ram T. rex below! This could be make it or break it, folks!

But its victory is short-lived when the dino is back on its feet as the two go nose-to-nose.

AND THE **WINNER** IS...

?

Make your choice, then turn to page 47 to find out what the experts think!

MAKE SOME NOISE FOR OUR CHAMPIONS!

What an ending! Ready to check out the hard-hitting results?

 WINNERS

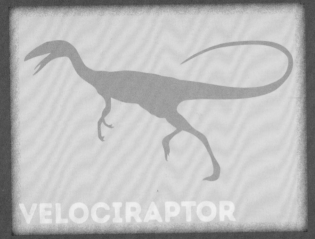

VELOCIRAPTOR

MOTORCYCLE

While both competitors put up a good show, it ultimately came down to speed—and Motorcycle powered on ahead!

ARGENTINOSAURUS

GARBAGE TRUCK

Argentinosaurus is our champ of chomping! Its appetite can't be beat. Aww, don't be so down in the dumps, Garbage Truck! You're still a hero to many.

WINNERS

TRICERATOPS

BULLDOZER

Triceratops's almighty horn broke Bulldozer's tire, making the machine unable to move, pinned it down for the big win!

STEGOSAURUS

EXCAVATOR

Excavator dug through to the treasure chest at the bottom of its trench! This machine was built to dig, while Stegosaurus just wasn't cut out for it. Better luck next time, Stegosaurus!

QUETZALCOATLUS

HELICOPTER

Quetzalcoatlus narrowly lossed to Helicopter, who was able to land on the hard-to-reach target. Quetzalcoatlus tried sticking the landing, but got stuck—and distracted by prey on the cliffside. Can you blame it? All that flying worked up an appetite!

WHO ELSE CAME OUT ON TOP?

Time to bring it home and reveal our final set of winners:

 WINNERS

SPINOSAURUS

TANK

Tank ended up on its back and tapped out, allowing Spinosaurus to pin it down for a victory! Spinosaurus was very tank-ful.

ICHTHYOSAUR

SUBMARINE

While Ichthyosaur could see better, Submarine was able to dive deeper and claimed the prize!

ANKYLOSAURUS

CRANE

It's a tie! Both dino and machine each wrecked their last obstacle at the same exact time. Soon after, Ankylosaurus got mad and climbed onto the wrecking ball. Let's just say it was more weight than Crane could bear, and the machine fell.

WINNERS

EDMONTOSAURUS

SNOWMOBILE

Edmontosaurus was so close until Snowmobile emerged and crossed the finish line. This dino isn't cut out for tests of speed.

T. REX

MONSTER TRUCK

T. rex came out on top as the reigning champ of the demolition derby! Monster Truck may have torn up the arena, but T. rex tore up Monster Truck.

WHO WAS YOUR MVP?

WHICH BATTLE WAS YOUR FAVORITE?

And there you have it! Dinosaurs and Machines really brought their A-game today for some incredible showstopping performances. Give it up for your favorites!

© 2020 Quarto Publishing Group USA Inc.
Published in 2020 by becker&mayer! kids, an imprint of The Quarto Group,
11120 NE 33rd Place, Suite 201, Bellevue, WA 98004 USA.
www.QuartoKnows.com

becker&mayer! kids titles are also available at discount for retail, wholesale, promotional, and bulk purchase. For details, contact the Special Sales Manager by email at specialsales@quarto.com or by mail at The Quarto Group, Attn: Special Sales Manager, 100 Cummings Center Suite 265D, Beverly, MA 01915 USA.

21 22 23 24 25   5 4 3 2 1

ISBN: 978-0-7603-7033-9

Digital edition published in 2021
eISBN: 978-0-7603-7034-6X

Library of Congress Cataloging-in-Publication Data available upon request.

Authors: Eric Geron
Illustration: Mat Edwards

Printed, manufactured, and assembled in Shanghai, China, 02/21.

Image credits: Design elements © Shutterstock.com

#334773